BENNY

Make Him glad!

the sad mad glad Christian

The Anatomy of Your Faith

Chuck Stump & Jim Strawn

ALWAYS HAVE Faith!!

Chuck Stump

Jim S

The Sad Mad Glad Christian-The Anatomy of Your Faith

For permissions, to order additional copies of this title, or to contact the authors, call or write:

Four Dolphins Press, LLC
P. O. Box 833
Scott Depot, West Virginia 25560
Phone (304) 757-8125

Visit our Web site at www.SadMadGladBooks.com

Printed in China at Everbest Printing Co.
Through Four Colour Imports, Louisville, Kentucky, USA

First Edition, September 2009

ISBN: 978-0-9799315-3-6

Four Dolphins Press would like to give the following people a *pat on the back* for *lending a helping hand*.

Graphic Design

Michael Teel and Jesse Corlis - Progressity, Inc., Charleston, West Virginia, www.Progressity.com

Editors

Nancy Wallace, Karen Reddick - The Red Pen Editor

Contributing Photographer

Steve Payne Photography, Charleston, West Virginia, www.StevePayne.com

Special thanks to:

Bill Ellis, Joe Jones, Chet Marshall, Chris Rogillio, Gina Rugeley and Dennis Sparks

This book is dedicated to our mothers,
Yvonne Fish Stump
and
Donna Margaret Strawn,
who introduced us to God when we were young.

About this book:

The Sad Mad Glad Christian – The Anatomy of Your Faith was created at the overwhelming request of many parents who bought our first books (**The Sad Mad Glad Book** and **Another Sad Mad Glad Book**) and wanted something with a distinctly spiritual message. This book was designed to excite children, to help them explore the Bible, and to help them learn to enjoy living life as Christians. The vibrant photos and rhymes that include American folk wisdom and common body idioms are the signature of the **Sad Mad Glad** series. This book adds thought-provoking questions and carefully selected scripture references that support each lesson. The discussions that arise from these reflection questions can be priceless. Please take time to read the scripture passages and to study the Word of God as you read this book. The Bible is an amazing book and, with so many scriptures to choose from, we're sure you can find additional scriptures that will add even more meaning to the messages and lessons.

The format of this book lends itself to Sunday school and home Bible study. You will find that the book has four distinct sections: Creation, Jesus and the Twelve Disciples, Symbols, and Habits (including stewardship, prayer, and forgiveness). These sections allow you to create your own series, such as children's sermons, Sunday school curriculum, or planned Bible studies.

Neither of us was formally educated in theology, but we are both parents who have been active in the church for as long as we can remember, and we want future generations to know how much it will mean to them to have God in their lives.

Please direct any comments or suggestions to:

Four Dolphins Press
P. O. Box 833
Scott Depot, WV 25560
Phone 304-757-8125
www.SadMadGladBooks.com

Our mothers put us **on the path.**

They'll forever be respected.

We went to church on Sundays.

God came first … that was expected.

That habit, learned while we were young,

sure laid a strong foundation,

and now we pass that lesson down

to future generations.

**Have you ever thought of the word "church" as a verb?
When people say they're going "to church," could it mean that they
are going "to pray," or "to worship?" What do you do at church?**

As **Christians,** we place **faith** in God,
the God of all creation.
We worship Jesus Christ,
who died ... and rose for our salvation.
We believe in the Holy Spirit,
who guides and empowers us all.
Sharing the love and grace of God
with others is our call.

John 3: 16-17

**God the Father, Jesus Christ, his son, and the Holy Spirit
are known as the three-in-one or the Trinity.**

And what is **faith?**
We're GLAD you asked.
It's to trust without a doubt.
You don't need proof or evidence –
that's what this book's about.

2 Corinthians 4: 16-18 | Hebrews 11

Faith is believing in something that you cannot see.
Can you think of some examples?

First we'll tell you how it started,
next Jesus Christ **takes center stage.**
Then symbols that you see and know
will be on every page.
As always we have pictures
that **will take your breath away.**
We'll finish up with how our **faith**
affects our lives today.

Romans 5: 1-5

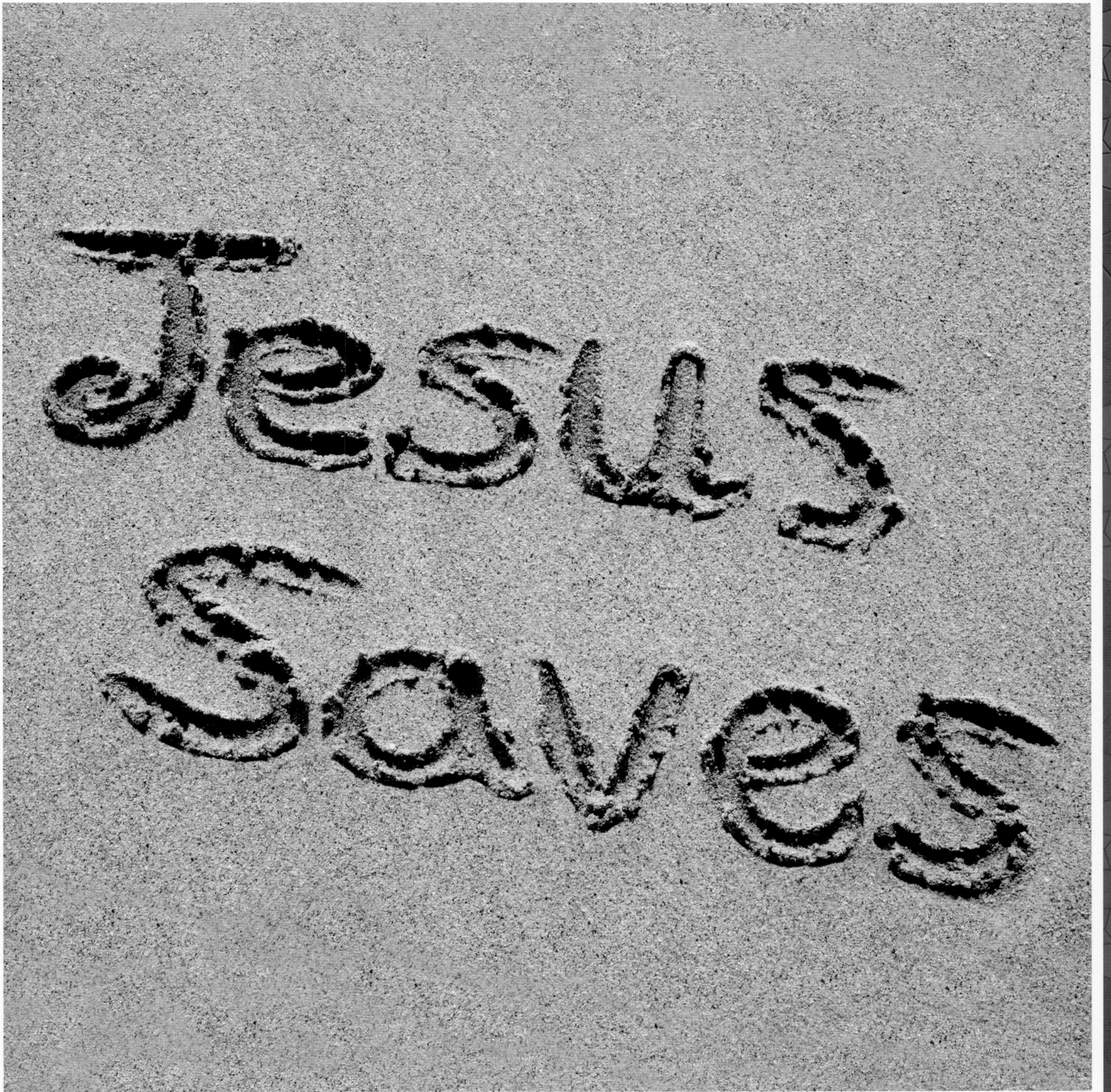
Jesus
Saves

Use this book with **your** Bible,

for it's there you'll find **the Word**

from Genesis to Revelation,

the way it all occurred.

You'll read of people and events

that happened long ago;

of Father, Son, and Spirit,

from whom all blessings flow.

John 1: 1-5, 14

The Bible is available in lots of different translations.

Which one do you use? Why?

The Bible is a special book;
it has so much to teach.
You need to keep it **close at hand**
and well **within your reach.**

Psalm 119: 105

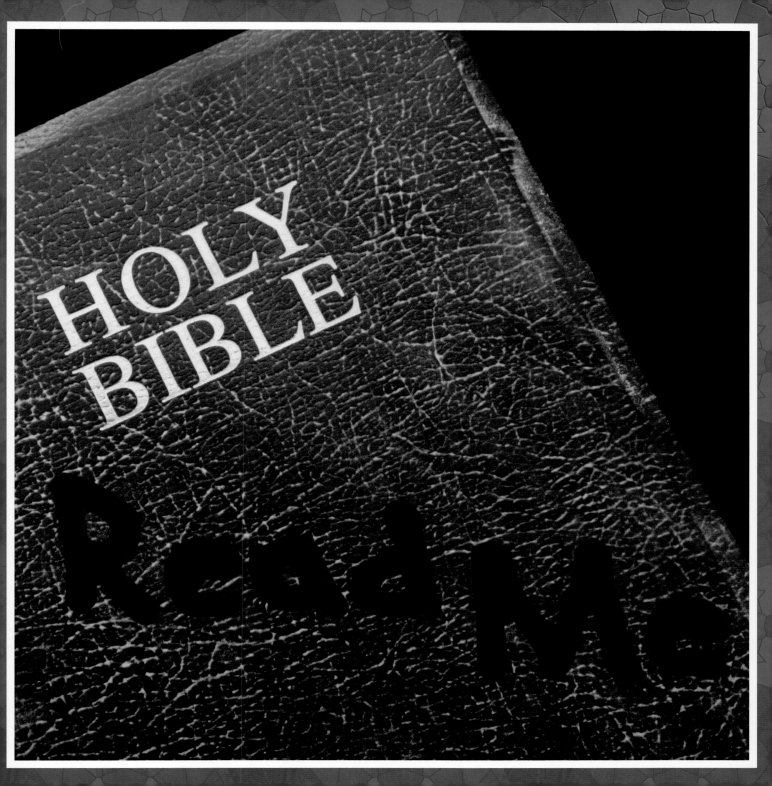

Your Bible tells heroic tales

of miracles, trips, and dreams,

of disciples, kings, and prophets,

and normal people too, it seems.

There's a great big fish, a burning bush,

and a giant nine feet tall,

lots of people (most related),

just no way to name them all.

Jonah | Exodus 3-4 | 1 Samuel 17

The Bible has 66 books. 39 are in the Old Testament and 27 are in the New Testament. Some Bibles include the 12 books of the Apocrypha, bringing the total to 78.

CREATION

Our God created everything

we smell, and touch, and see.

You might say He had His **hands full,**

from the sky down to the sea.

In six short days He finished.

He'd done all that He would.

God looked around and He was GLAD,

and said that **it was good.**

Genesis 1 | Psalm 104

What do you think are some of God's coolest creations?

On the seventh day He rested.

He tells us to do the same -

to dedicate this day to Him

and praise His holy name.

Where two or more are gathered,

God will GLADLY meet you there.

Your presence is what matters most,

no matter what you wear.

Genesis 2: 2-3 | Exodus 20: 8-11

The first people God made were Adam and Eve.

They were approached by an evil snake.

They didn't **use their heads** … and sinned.

WOW! What a big mistake!

They felt guilty about the fruit they ate;

they'd fallen from God's graces.

They left the garden with **heavy hearts.**

It was **written all over their faces.**

Genesis 3

We all are tempted by sin.

What can we learn from Adam and Eve?

And soon things went from bad to worse.
God was **MAD!** He felt betrayed.
He decided He would flood the earth
and destroy all He had made.
God asked Noah to build an ark.
Noah became God's **right-hand man.**
He took in the animals two by two
before the rain began.

Genesis 6:5 – 7:5

**People thought Noah was out of his mind when he was building the ark, but he did what God asked him to do.
What do you think Noah was thinking?**

For forty days and forty nights
it rained, and rained, and rained.
When everything was said and done,
only Noah's ark remained.

Genesis 7:6 – 9:17

The ark was bigger than a football field!
It was 450 feet long, 75 feet wide and 45 feet high.

God decided He must have some rules.
They became the **law of the land.**
If you think they don't apply today,
your **head is buried in the sand!**

Exodus 19:16 - 20:17

How many of the Ten Commandments can you list?

**When you study the Ten Commandments,
how do you think they apply to our daily lives?**

לא תרצח   אנכי יהוה

לא תנאף   לא יהיה

לא תגנב   לא תשא את

לא תענה   זכור את יום

לא תחמד   כבד את אביך

Let's jump ahead a few thousand years,
or we'll have too many pages.
Straight to **the** event that changed all time…
it's a story for the ages.

JESUS and the TWELVE DISCIPLES

Jesus Christ was born to save us all.

It's through Him, we **see the light.**

It all began in Bethlehem

on a dark December night.

He was born of the Virgin Mary,

(conceived by the Holy Spirit).

The story has angels and a wondrous star.

You'll **get chills** each time you hear it!

Luke 2: 1-21

What is your favorite part of the Christmas story?

We gather on **Christmas** to celebrate, sometimes **losing sight** of the reason. So remember, without the birth of Christ, there'd be no Christmas season!

**When someone says "Christmas"
what is the first thing that comes to mind?**

To prove Jesus was the **Messiah,**
God gave Him the power to heal.
The lame would walk, the deaf would hear,
to show God's power was real.
Once Jesus met a blind man
who made a pitiful cry.
This healing led to the popular phrase
"Dear friend, **here's mud in your eye.**"

Mark 5: 21-43 | John 9: 1-11

Jesus healed lots of people in the Bible.

How many stories of healing can you find?

Jesus recruited twelve disciples
and He put them on the road.
The only thing they carried
were the powers He'd bestowed.
In the **blink of an eye,** four fishermen
dropped their nets to answer His call.
His friends would soon be **fishers of men,**
heads held high and **standing tall.**

Matthew 10: 1-14 | Mark 1: 16-20

**Can you name the twelve disciples
who committed their lives to Jesus?**

Andrew, the first one on our list,

was one of Jesus' closest friends.

Simon Peter, Andrew's brother,

was "the Rock" right to the end.

John, known as the "Apostle of Love,"

was also the brother of James.

"Doubting **Thomas**" was courageous,

although he questioned many things.

Matthew, the tax collector,

had more money than the rest.

Bartholomew was skinned alive.

That's what history suggests.

There were *two* disciples
who went by **James.**
They were both devoted and calm.
Judas gave Christ **the kiss of death**
after the High Priest **greased his palm.**
Legend says **Thaddeus** was a shepherd
who paid homage that first December.
Philip and **Simon** the Zealot
are the others to remember.

Luke 22: 1-6 | Mark 14: 43-46

**The High Priest gave Judas 30 pieces of
silver for turning Jesus over to be crucified.**

Their job – to help Him spread the word.
They received, so they gave without pay.
Now it's time for us to **shoulder the load**
and be disciples for Him today!

Matthew 28: 16-20 | Luke 9: 23

What do you think it means to be a "disciple?"

God appointed Jesus as the judge

of the living and the dead.

After all He once was human,

so He knows what's **in your head.**

We need to look to Him for strength.

We're tempted every day,

and Jesus knows just what it takes

to turn and walk away.

Matthew 4: 1-11 | 1 Corinthians 10: 13

Jesus lived on earth for 33 years.

He experienced every temptation but never sinned.

E COMPLIR A L

NOLI HANDE

RES JOSEP DA

EF JESÚS PERO

NARA PILATA AUTO

EL SEU COS DE

A ACCEDIR JOSE

RE DE LA CREU

SYMBOLS

Our **faith** has many symbols,

like the colors in the sky

that God put in the rainbow

once the flood passed Noah by.

God was SAD and had a **second thought;**

maybe the flood was too severe.

When we see a rainbow overhead,

it reminds us He is near.

Genesis 8: 20-22 | Genesis 9: 8-17

Where were you the last time you saw a rainbow?

When a dove is a part of the story,

the Holy Spirit is in our midst.

Of all the symbols in the Bible,

it holds a special place on the list.

On the day that Jesus was baptized

God's spirit appeared as a dove.

John the Baptist was very GLAD

when he saw it come down from above.

Genesis 8: 8-12 | Matthew 3: 16

Water plays an enormous role
when we baptize in God's name.
Jesus **walked on the water**
and helped Peter do the same.

Matthew 14: 22-33 | John 13: 3-15

Jesus used it to wash the disciples' feet.

Moses parted a sea down the middle.

Jesus turned the water into wine.

That's a fact and not a riddle.

Without it we would have no life;

without it plants can't grow.

We see it when we're SAD ... as tears

when the **healing waters** flow.

John 2 | John 3 | Exodus 14-15 | Matthew 5: 4

How many Bible stories can you remember that have water in them?

Early **Christians** could be put to death,

so they had to sneak around.

They'd draw this symbol on their homes

or sometimes on the ground.

Wherever they saw an **icthus**

they were safe and **in good hands.**

This symbol means the same today.

It's on lots of cars and vans.

Icthus (or ixthus) is an acrostic meaning
"Jesus Christ, God's son is our savior."

I = Iesous = **Jesus**   **C** = Christos = **Christ**

TH = Theou = **God's**   **U** = Uiou = **Son**   **S** = Sotor = **Savior**

When you hear the words

"He died for us,"

think of sacrifice and compassion.

Jesus died to save us from our sins

in a very painful fashion.

John 19

Since Jesus' crucifixion, the cross has become the most widely recognized symbol of the Christian faith. At least two disciples, Peter and Andrew, were also crucified, one on a cross shaped like an "X", the other upside down.

But there's something else you need to know,

a happy ending to this story.

The third day His grave was empty.

He conquered death and rose in glory!

Mark 16

Easter is the annual celebration of Jesus Christ's being raised from the dead. Just as spring signals the end of winter, Easter reminds us that Christ rose into heaven, where He reigns with God.

We celebrate communion
with the symbols of bread and wine.
We remember **why** Christ died for us,
and of his love divine.
The *need* to love runs through us all;
handed down from God above.
For Jesus it just comes naturally…
it is truly **in his blood.**

Mark 14: 22-24

God's messengers are **angels.**

Believe with **faith** that they exist.

Some say they've even seen them -

others claim that they've been **"kissed."**

They foretold the birth of Jesus.

They appeared in many dreams.

They announced the resurrection.

Sometimes single. Some in teams.

Psalm 91: 11 | Hebrews 13: 2

Angels are mentioned 299 times in the Bible!

We know that angels are at work
when there's **more than meets the eye.**
They leave no proof or evidence –
just a sense **faith** can't deny.

Hebrews 13: 2

Did you realize you have a Guardian Angel?

HABITS

Let's take a look at habits
that all Christians **take to heart.**
To do these things will demonstrate to God
you're trying to do your part.

Your goal is to read each habit

and then see how it applies.

Let's check the life you're living.

Is it pleasing **in God's eyes?**

Do you **put your best foot forward**

and set examples every day?

Do you share your **faith** with others

so that they might know the way?

Hebrews 13: 15-16

**The Helix nebula, known by scientists
as the "Eye of God," is 650 light years away.**

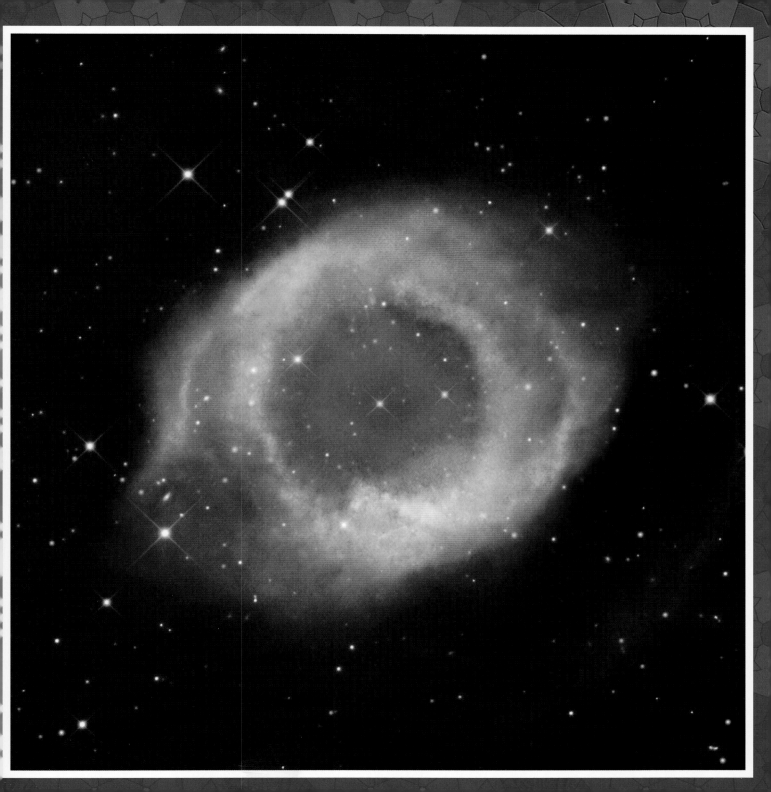

Enthusiasm is an old Greek word.
"In God" is its definition.
With God you'll have the strength each day
to follow your ambition.
You must be **bright-eyed and bushy-tailed**
when it's time for worship and prayers,
and be willing **to go the extra mile**
to tell others how much God cares.

We love **random acts of kindness.**
Do at least one every day.
You can always **lend a helping hand;**
the *Good Samaritan* showed the way!
You might call a friend who's lonely,
or share your stuff with one who's poor.
You might think to cut your neighbor's grass
or run ahead to hold the door.

Luke 10: 29-37

True **stewards** have a **heart of gold,**

not falling prey to envy and greed.

They're grateful for what God's given them

and keep only what they *need.*

It's not just about their money

but their time and talents, too!

Some of them really **tighten their belts**

and do **ALL** that they can do.

Luke 21:1-4

**How do you share your time, talents,
and treasures with the Lord?**

God loves a cheerful giver;

think *abundance*…don't think *lack*.

Don't be afraid to give someone

the shirt right off your back!

2 Corinthians 9: 6-8

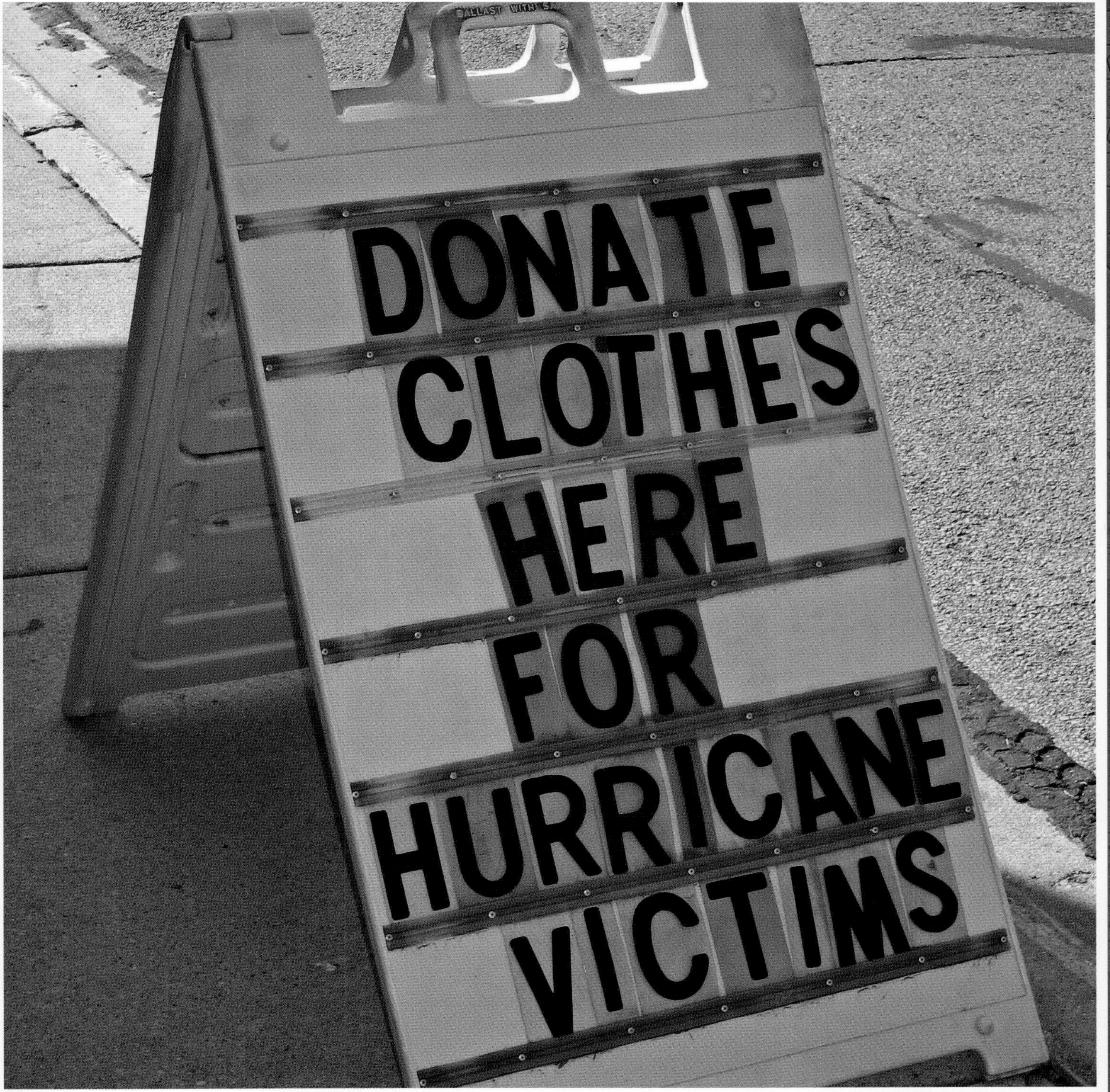
DONATE
CLOTHES
HERE
FOR
HURRICANE
VICTIMS

There's another job for **stewards;**

it's to take care of our planet each day.

God has given us *everything* we need,

so we can't throw it all away.

Our planet is very fragile.

All of the systems are connected.

We have to work together

to make sure it's all protected!

Genesis 1: 29-30

What do you do to help protect our planet?

When you find your **back against the wall,**

find a quiet place and pray.

Ask the *Trinity* for guidance,

and feel your worries melt away.

Matthew 6: 6 | Luke 11: 1-4

You won't get everything you _want_,

but God **will** meet your _needs_.

Cool your heels, be very patient,

and just follow as He leads.

James 1: 2-3, 12 | Philippians 4: 19

Some prayers may seem unanswered,

but remember, God knows best.

When we pray for things that make Him **GLAD,**

He'll honor our request.

Luke 18: 1-8 | Deuteronomy 4: 7 |Colossians 1: 9-14

Whenever God is present,

He creates real **"peace of mind."**

You need to know that those who seek

are surely those who find.

Matthew 7: 7-8 | Psalm 46:10

Daily prayer and reflection bring us closer to God.

When do you make time to pray?

An eye for an eye and a tooth for a tooth

is the way some think today.

It might be very popular,

but it isn't Jesus' way.

It's easy for you to love your friends,

but bullies are hard to forgive.

Once you learn to **turn the other cheek,**

you can really start to live.

Luke 6: 27-29 | Matthew 18: 21-22

How do you let someone know that you have forgiven them?

With **all your heart** and **all your mind** and **all your strength and soul,**

that's how you are to love the Lord.

That is your daily goal.

God made us in His image,

to love others as He loves us.

It's a job we should be GLAD to do –

and do without a fuss.

Matthew 22: 37-39

What can we do to show God that we love others as He loves us?

Our **faith** is full of mystery.

Sometimes we ask, "*Why* is there **bad?**"

Well, without **bad,** we can't have **good,**

without **sad,** we can't have **glad.**

We can't have **life** unless there's **death,**

or **wrong** unless there's **right.**

We can't have **love** unless there's **hate,**

or **dark** unless there's **light.**

We can't have **rich** unless there's **poor.**

Some **give** while others **take.**

Your Christian life will be defined

by the choices that **you** make.

Ecclesiastes 3: 1-8

What if someone **hasn't seen the light?**

What if someone's full of greed?

What if they **stabbed you in the back**

to ensure that they'd succeed?

Can they still become a Christian?

Will God forgive them for their past?

With a **change of heart** they could repent

and be part of our cast.

To accept Jesus as their savior

is all they would need to do.

Whenever someone **sees the light,**

their life can be renewed.

Psalms 51: 10-12 | Romans 8: 38-39 | Romans 10: 10-11

God knows **each hair upon your head** and **every breath you take,**

every thought you've ever had,

and every move you make.

Your thoughts and moves define your **faith.**

and God is there to aid.

With Him, **you'll never walk alone,**

so you shouldn't be afraid.

Psalm 23 | Matthew 10: 30 | Jeremiah 1: 5

When do you feel that God is looking over your shoulder?

Our lives are **footprints in the sand,**

some day to be erased.

We'll be measured by the deeds we've done

and the challenges we've faced.

Don't ever let it **slip your mind:**

God has a master plan.

You'll see a wave come rolling in,

and He'll gently **take your hand.**

Jeremiah 29: 11

He'll lead you to that special place -

His Kingdom up above.

You'll finally meet Him **face to face...**

and know eternal Love.

1 Corinthians 2: 9 | Revelation 21: 1-4

The End

We would like to know what you think.
Go to **www.SadMadGladBooks.com**
and send us your Book Report.

Thanks!

Chuck   *Jim*